Written by Whitney Hickerson

Illustrated by Caitlyn Vega

Annette & Frankie Publishing
First Edition, United States 2024
ISBN 979-8-218-47433-1
Copyright © 2024 by Whitney Hickerson

Written by Whitney Hickerson
Illustrated by Caitlyn Vega
Cover Design and Layout by Whitney Hickerson
Edited by Whitney and Justin Hickerson

The text for this book was set in Over the Rainbow. The illustrations were rendered digitally.

This book was written to allow the title of Mommy as the reader to be replaced with any other title of a family member or other loved one who wishes to read to a special baby.

All rights reserved. This book or any portion thereof may not be reproduced or used in any manner whatsoever without the express written permission of the Author.

For book orders or inquiries regarding special discounts or donations, please contact:
annettefrankiepublishing@gmail.com

to the babies that made me a Mommy

Hi my sweet baby
I'm excited to talk to you
I prayed and prayed
and now you're here
I'm your Mommy
I love you

you're so little
so fragile
but I'm already yours
I'm wrapped around your finger
my sweet boy or girl

I take you everywhere
you're such a great helper
I love everything more now
because we do it together

I'm so glad God chose
you for me and me for you
I close my eyes and picture
the big day I'll meet you

I can't wait to see your eyes looking back at me

I can't wait to hear your
voice when you giggle or sing

I can't wait to hold your hand
and see what you will do

I can't wait to kiss your toes
and see where you will go

I pray that you keep growing
so big and so strong
But I know that where God has us today
is right where we belong

www.ingramcontent.com/pod-product-compliance
Lightning Source LLC
Chambersburg PA
CBHW042055050526
44107CB00110B/1186